Pebble® Plus

HOW **ELECTRICITY** GETS FROM **POWER PLANTS** TO **HOMES**

by Megan Cooley Peterson

Consultant: A. David Salvia
Assistant Professor, Electrical Engineering
Penn State, University Park, Pennsylvania

raintree
a Capstone company — publishers for children

Raintree is an imprint of Capstone Global Library Limited, a company incorporated in England and Wales having its registered office at 264 Banbury Road, Oxford, OX2 7DY – Registered company number: 6695582

www.raintree.co.uk
myorders@raintree.co.uk

Edited by Jill Kalz
Designed by Juliette Peters and Katelin Plekkenpol
Picture research by Morgan Walters
Production by Tori Abraham
Originated by Capstone Global Library Limited
Printed and bound in China.

ISBN 978 1 474 71319 1
20 19 18 17 16
10 9 8 7 6 5 4 3 2 1

British Library Cataloguing in Publication Data
A full catalogue record for this book is available from the British Library.

Acknowledgements
We would like to thank the following for permission to reproduce photographs: Capstone Studio: Karon Dubke, 21; Shutterstock: Chones, 17, chungking, 7, Concept Photo, 20, CoolKengzz, 6, Dmitry Kalinovsky, 14, DomDew_Studio, 18, Givaga, 1, back cover, Innershadows Photography, Cover, jakit17, 13, Karkas, 8, leisuretime70, 12, m.jrn, 10, Martin Capek, (blue lightning) top right Cover, (transformer) top left Cover, 5, michaeljung, 15, Rido, 19, rtem, 9, Sergey Nivens, 3, Shooting Star Studio, 16, ssguy, 11, tab62, Cover, wang song, 22-23

Every effort has been made to contact copyright holders of material reproduced in this book. Any omissions will be rectified in subsequent printings if notice is given to the publisher.

All the internet addresses (URLs) given in this book were valid at the time of going to press. However, due to the dynamic nature of the internet, some addresses may have changed, or sites may have changed or ceased to exist since publication. While the author and publisher regret any inconvenience this may cause readers, no responsibility for any such changes can be accepted by either the author or the publisher.

CONTENTS

Where electricity comes from

Electricity is a form of energy that makes things work. It powers TVs, lights and much more. Where does electricity come from?

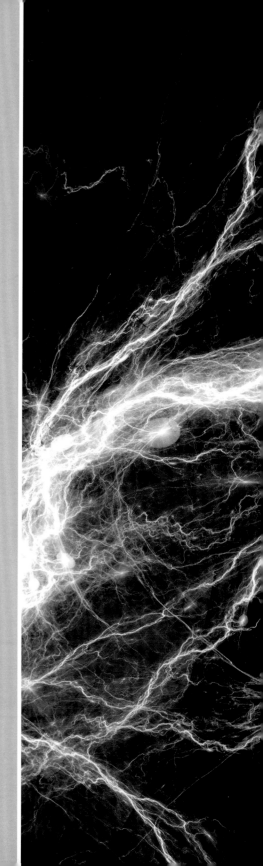

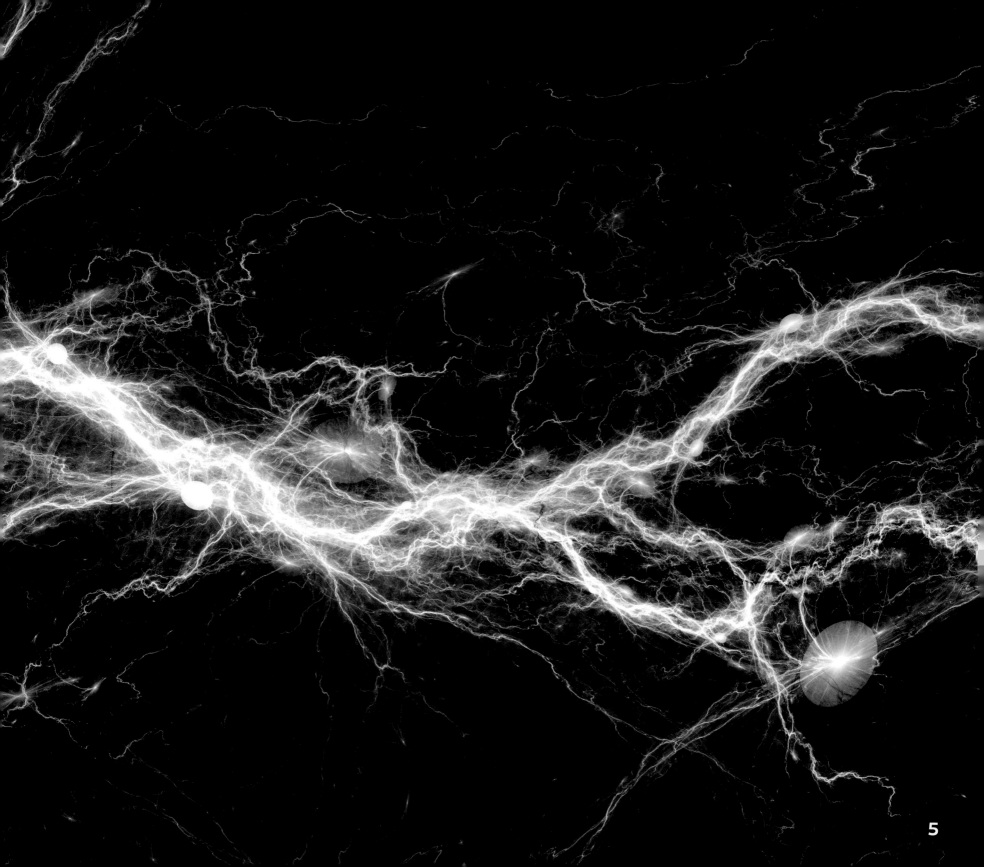

Power plants make electricity.
They make it in different ways.
One type of power plant
boils water. The water turns
into steam.

boiler

Hiss! The steam rises quickly.

It turns a turbine. A turbine

is a large wheel with blades.

The turbine turns a generator.

The generator makes electricity.

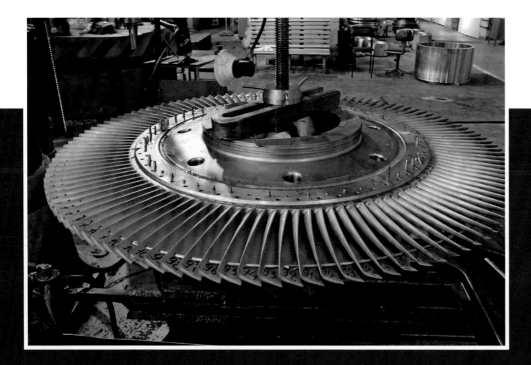

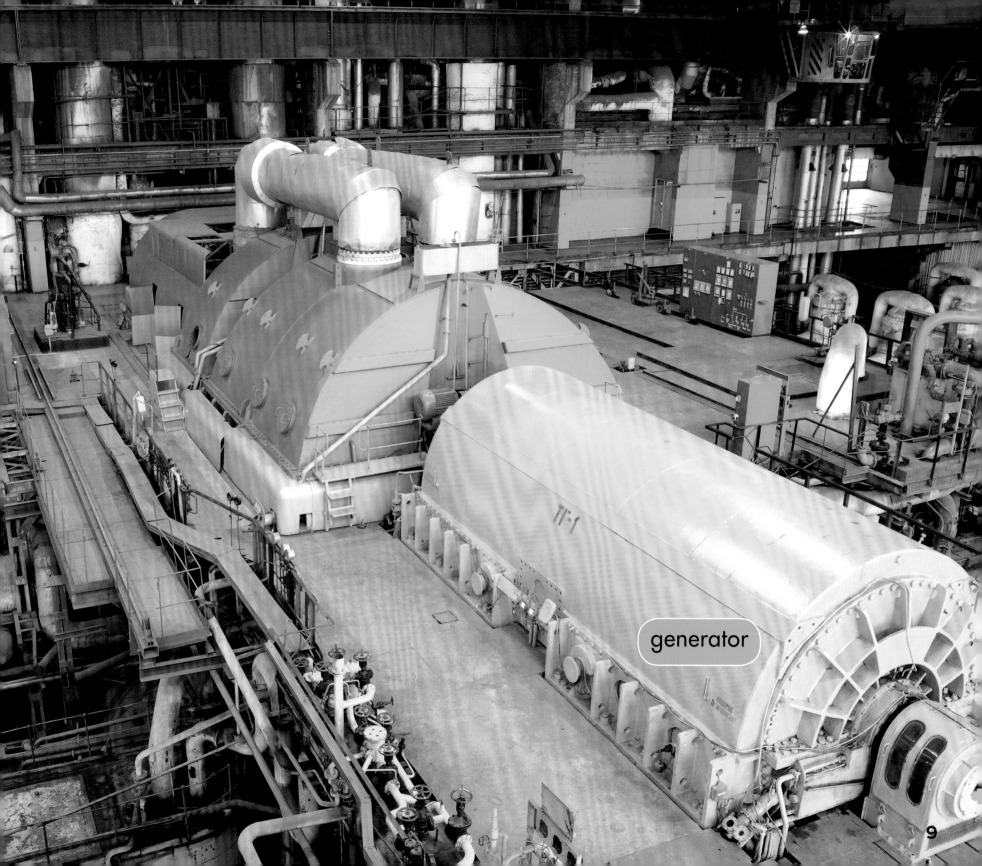

generator

How electricity moves

Electricity moves through

metal wires called power lines.

Some power lines hang in the air.

Others are buried under ground.

The electricity in power lines
is dangerous to touch.
Transformers make electricity safer
to use before it enters buildings.

transformers

transformers

Electricity at home

Electricians install wires for electricity inside buildings. They wear rubber shoes and gloves for safety. The rubber protects the electricians from shocks.

Electricity flows through plug sockets in walls. When you plug something in, electricity makes it work. Press a switch. Zing! A lightbulb turns on!

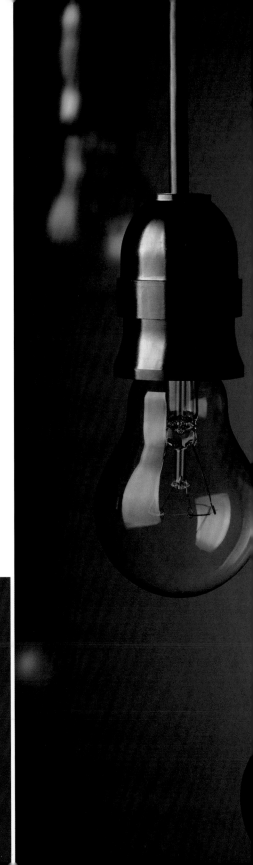

A meter measures how much
electricity people use.
People pay for the amount
of electricity they use.

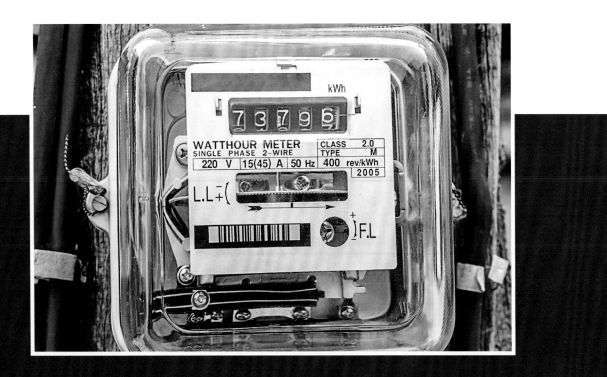

Saving electricity

You can do your part

to save electricity. Watch less

TV. Play fewer video games.

Turn off the lights when

you leave a room.

GLOSSARY

boil heat water or another liquid until it bubbles; water gives off steam when it boils

electrician someone who puts in and fixes electrical wiring in a building

electricity natural force that can be used to make light and heat or to make machines work

energy ability to do work, such as moving things or giving heat or light

generator machine that produces electricity by turning a magnet inside a coil of wire

install put in and connect for use

measure find out the size or strength of something

meter machine that keeps track of how much electricity a home or business uses

power plant building or group of buildings used to make electricity; some power plants burn coal or gas, while others use water, wind or sunshine to make electricity

steam gas that water turns into when it boils

transformer device that connects power lines to buildings

turbine engine powered by steam, water, wind or gas passing across the blades of a fanlike device and making it spin

BOOKS

Electricity (How Does My Home Work?), Chris Oxlade (Heinemann Educational Books, 2012)

Exploring Electricity (A Sense of Science), Claire Llewellyn (Franklin Watts, 2012)

Moving up with Science: Electricity, Peter Riley (Franklin Watts, 2015)

WEBSITES

www.bbc.co.uk/education/clips/zcnhfg8
This video clip shows how electricity gets to our homes.

www.bbc.co.uk/guides/z96ckqt
Find out what we use electricity for and how to stay safe around electricity.

www.switchedonkids.org.uk/
This site tells you all about electricity and how to use it safely.

CRITICAL THINKING QUESTIONS

1. Electricity travels through power lines. Why do you think power lines hang high in the air or lie underground?

2. Explain why electricians are important. What might happen if there were no electricians?

3. Name two things you can do to save electricity.

INDEX